JOE BRAINS

by Nat Gabriel
illustrated by Adam Gordon

Scott Foresman

Editorial Offices: Glenview, Illinois • New York, New York
Sales Offices: Reading, Massachusetts • Duluth, Georgia
Glenview, Illinois • Carrollton, Texas • Menlo Park, California

Joe Barnes stood in front of his class reading the end of his essay out loud. "The 1960s was a time of great music. People wrote songs about peace, love, and ending racial hostility. However, America was not such a peaceful place. The hateful shadow of prejudice fell across the land." Joe read the last line of his paper and then looked up at his teacher, Mr. Haze.

"That is a very good way of saying it, Joe. 'The hateful shadow of prejudice.' Very good. Wouldn't you agree, class? Excellent work, Mr. Barnes."

Joe felt proud when Mr. Haze praised his paper. He had put a great deal of effort into it. He enjoyed writing, and he liked Mr. Haze too. The bell rang, and Joe gathered his books and papers. He had to be in gym class in five minutes, but first he stopped at his locker to get his sneakers.

"Hey, Joe Brains! Do you want me to shine your glasses for you?" someone shouted from across the hall.

Joe recognized that voice. He closed his eyes and took a deep breath.

"No thanks, Boone," he said.

"What did you say? I couldn't hear you," said Boone. He walked over and lay his heavy arm across Joe's shoulder. Although there was no hostility in Boone's voice, Joe didn't trust him.

"No thank you," said Joe in a louder voice. "And it's Barnes, not Brains."

"Aw, come on—be a sport. I'll polish up your glasses, and in return you can write my prejudice essay. It's so easy for you. I bet you could do it with your eyes closed."

"Then why would I need my glasses cleaned?" said Joe as he opened his locker.

Then the bell rang and they hustled off to gym.

It was the third week of school. Joe was new to the school because his family had just moved to town. He hadn't made any real friends yet. He thought it was hateful the way that new kids were treated at school. Boone was the only one who had taken any interest in him—and it didn't seem like a very good match. Joe was an excellent student while Boone never raised his hand in class. The only thing Boone liked about school was gym, but that was Joe's least favorite part of the day.

Most of the boys were bigger and faster than Joe. When they picked teams, Joe was always the last one to be chosen. It wasn't that Joe was bad at sports. In fact he was a pretty good basketball player. He and his father would shoot hoops most nights after dinner. But for some reason, the kids at school just assumed he wasn't any good at sports. They got a kick out of heaping verbal abuse on Joe. They called him "Egghead" and "Professor" and, of course, "Joe Brains." They never passed him the ball, so he never got a chance to show them he could play.

Joe wished the boys could see that he wasn't as different from them as they thought. Sure, he was smart, but that didn't mean he couldn't play ball. People who wore glasses and read books could still make lay-ups. He was living proof of that.

After gym came lunch. Joe always brought his lunch from home and sat at the corner table reading a book while he ate.

"Hey, Joe Brains. Do you mind if I join you?" asked Boone.

"Only if you quit that name-calling and abuse," replied Joe.

Joe looked up as Boone pulled out his chair and sat down.

"May I ask you something?" Boone asked.

"Go ahead," said Joe as he took a bite of his sandwich.

"Why are smart people bad at sports?" said Boone.

"Who says they are?" answered Joe.

"It's a fact. Everybody knows it's true," said Boone.

"Well, I happen to know it's not true," said Joe. "Meet me in the gym after school, and I'll prove it."

When the final bell rang, Joe headed to the gym. Boone wasn't there yet, so he picked up a basketball and began to shoot baskets. He shot the ball into the basket over and over. Sometimes he missed and it bounced off the rim. Most of the time, though, he sank his shots perfectly. He was so busy shooting that he didn't hear Boone come in.

"You're not bad for a smart guy," said Boone.

"Come on. Let's play one-on-one," replied Joe.

"You're on, Mr. Brains," said Boone.

The two boys played for a long time. Boone was better than Joe, but Joe still managed to sink his share of baskets. Finally they felt exhausted and sat down on the floor.

"So, do you still think that smart people are bad at sports?" asked Joe.

Boone shook his head.

"Do you want to play some more?"

"No, I have to go. I have to write that essay for tomorrow," said Boone.

"What are you going to write about?" asked Joe.

"You'll see," smiled Boone.

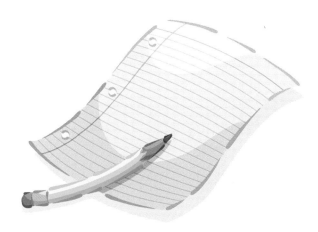

In class the next day, Mr. Haze asked which students would volunteer to read their essays out loud. Boone raised his hand.

"Well, well," said Mr. Haze with a big smile, "you may go first, Boone."

Boone nodded and walked to the front of the room. He cleared his throat and began to read. "Prejudice is all about people thinking people are different when they're really not. Maybe they're a different color, or they speak a different language. But inside people are just people. If you want to get rid of prejudice, you have to start by learning one important thing—what you think is true may not be true at all!"

Boone read the entire essay in a loud, clear voice. When he finished, Mr. Haze clapped his hands.

"That was great," he said. "I especially liked the example of the boy with glasses who gets picked last for the basketball team. That was a very original way of demonstrating prejudice."

Boone smiled a smile so big it almost didn't fit on his face.

After class, Joe went to his locker to get his sneakers for gym. He looked across the hall for Boone, but he wasn't there. Joe wanted to tell him what a good job he'd done on his essay.

When he got to the gym, Boone was already there. He was warming up with some of the other boys.

"Okay, gentlemen. Line up," called the teacher. "Pick your teams and let's get started."

Boone had the first pick. He picked Joe. A couple of the boys laughed, but Boone smiled and slapped Joe on the back.

"We'll show them," he said.

It was the best game of basketball Joe had ever played. For the first time he felt that he was really part of the game. When the bell rang at the end of class, Joe was sorry that it was over.

As Boone and Joe left the gym, one of the other boys called out to Joe. "Basketball tryouts are after school today, Joe. Are you going to come?"

"He'll be there!" Boone answered for him.

"Thanks for picking me today," said Joe.

"No problem. Thanks for giving me the idea for my essay. I got an A," said Boone.

"Great," said Joe.

Maybe they weren't such a bad match after all, Joe thought as he and his friend headed off to lunch.